The Greatest Game on Earth

A Collection of Footballing Verse

© 2007 Emdad Rahman
http://www.Emdad.NeemIT.net

Published by Ashwood House Publishing Ltd
7 Durham Way, Rotherham S62 6FL, UK
(01709) 528 528

info@ashwood-house.com
http://www.Ashwood-House.com
http://www.Football-Poems.com

ISBN-10: 0-9554873-2-3
ISBN-13: 978-0-9554873-2-3

All rights reserved. No part of this publication may be reproduced, stored in a retrieval system, or transmitted, in any form or by any means, electronic, mechanical, photocopying, recording and/or otherwise, without prior written permission of the copyright holder.

THE GREATEST GAME ON EARTH

A COLLECTION OF FOOTBALLING VERSE

*To Zain
Best regards*

EMDAD RAHMAN

"If there are still people around who think football is just 90 minutes of chasing a ball around, then Emdad Rahman's book should put them right. With Nessun Dorma, Pavarotti and Grand Opera already on the terraces, it was only a matter of time till poetry moved in.

'The Greatest Game on Earth' adds the stanza to soccer's cultural bonanza."

Ralph Windle, otherwise known as Bertie Ramsbottom
British poet, writer and presenter
Editor of "The Poetry of Business Life"

"Emdad has lived up to his promise of providing an uplifting book of poetry. This collection of verse is inspiring.

'The Greatest Game on Earth' is a stimulated and reassured compilation, amusing, gloomy, consistently proficient."

Muhib Choudhury
President of British Bangladesh Press Club

"Vigorous, startling, expressive, poignant and subtle. Emdad's knowledge of the beautiful game is immense and the book is testament to that. He cleverly informs the reader of past and present history and educates us in a pleasurable way. For some it will be a trip down memory lane, from remembering that night in Istanbul to Scholes' failed upper cuts.

This is a must read for all football fans. I enjoyed the book – it is easy to read, exciting and well written. Five stars for a five star writer."

Shakayet Hussain
General Secretary & Co-founder of United Sporting Luton FC

"Humorous, touching and most of all engaging. A poignant expression of yearnings, memories and joy. Football needed just that poetic touch!"

Rabina Khan
Author of "Rainbow Hands" & "Ayesha's Rainbow"

"I believe that everybody would benefit from a daily poetry fix. This book contains well crafted and wholesome poetry. Congratulations go to the author on his writing debut."

Shafiqul Haque
Mayor of the London Borough of Tower Hamlets 2006/07

"This is an extension of Emdad's talents – that were evident from our time together as classmates in secondary school. This book comes highly recommended."

Abdal Ullah
President of Stepney Football Club

"A collection of stimulating poems."

Councillor Rania Khan

"I wish Emdad well with his new book. It's always good to see Tower Hamlets citizens engaged in cultural activities especially in publishing."

Jim Fitzpatrick MP

Dedication

Dedicated to my three tigers: Ismael, Talha and Hamza.

Big up to Anisa, Shakila, Zakia, Nadia, Wasif, Jamila, Abbas, Yusuf, Osman and Danyal.

A mention also to the memory of little Umar Qureishi.

Man is most nearly himself when he achieves the seriousness of a child at play – Heraclitus.

Contents

Foreword 1
Introduction 3

El Diego's boots 7
Hot air bag 8
Remembering Wharton 9
Bust that onion bag 11
Dirt free Harry 12
Evertonian ecstasy 13
'Lurch' makes history 14
Jumping Jackflashes 15
Schole in the hole 16
Marc Vivien Foe   1975 – 2003 17
A summer's night in Istanbul 18
Video nasty! 21
Monsieur Wenger's Rage 23
Little & Large Show 24
The Major's last stand 25
FC Carra & Gerry 26
Wanderers Wonderland 27
The silent king 28
Poland's Montgomery – Acrostic homage to Dudek! 29
The devil incarnate 30
Redemption 31
Iron man or Psycho 32
Sweet Liverpool 33
Cashley Cole 34
Il Capitano of the Nerazzuri 35
Davide Pleate 36
And Sheva must score 37
The Laird from Govan 38
Gladiator Tardelli's Passion 39
Red Army! 41
Blunt Macca 42
Professor screwball and his madcap boots 43

The Lisbon Lions	44
The Iceman	45
The Magnificent Magyars	47
Fergie's bridesmaids	50
Athens 2007	51
Reversing fortune	52
Gross judgemental error	53
Athina 2007	55
Milanese hit Haiku	56
Allemagne Acrostic	57
Brilliant Orange	59
Combat with Lawro	60

Foreword

Bill Shankly once said, "Football's not a matter of life and death – it's more important than that."

The global football industry is a monster enterprise, an unstoppable juggernaut that is going from strength to strength. Football in England in the shape of the Premiership has become a phenomenon. Fans are flocking to grounds, superstars are arriving en masse and our papers, inboxes and cell phones are brimming with the most up to date news and supplements.

The incredulous amongst us may see poetry and football as incompatible, yet not so well known is the fact that a number of our football clubs now have football poets in residence.

In the words of Michael Horowitz, "Football and poetry have a lot in common: they are performance arts with more socially communicative panache than many other forms of entertainment or competition – though of course both provide superlative entertainment too."

I am delighted to have been offered the opportunity to write the foreword for this book of football verse. I taught the author when he was a pupil at Stepney Green Boys School, East London between 1988 and 1992. Football is a sport that produces the correct doses of drama, heartache, jubilation and ecstasy; absolutely key elements for a poem to stimulate and to inspire the masses.

The book is an endowment from the author and it contains verses that will touch a chord with poetry and football lovers alike. As a mainstream school teacher I would encourage the use of such forms of poetry in educational institutes, to help foster methods of communication. Related workshops would also be a useful tool to boost self-esteem in pupils.

The book has touched on different aspects of the beautiful game; Diego Maradona, childhood dreams, Christian Gross, Dave Beasant's historical penalty save and Istanbul 2005, where the family of football, bar the Milanese witnessed and celebrated the most amazing European night of all.

The author is a popular name within his community, and this in itself should be enough to create interest and get people to pick up and read the book.

This book will take you on a journey, from theatrics to the spectacular, from the dire and dour to sheer magnificence. For all lovers of poetry and football this short collection will ignite treasured recollections and reminiscences of the beautiful game. If you're into the artistic aspect of football, here's something that is sure to delight and captivate you.

Chris Kinnear

Manager: Margate FC, 1997 – 2006
Manager: Dover FC, 1986 – 1996
Teacher at Stepney Green Maths & Computing College (Formerly Stepney Green School for Boys)

Introduction

"Football is a global language. It can bridge social, cultural and religious divides. It enhances personal development and growth, teaches us teamwork and fair play, builds self-esteem and opens doors to new opportunities. This, in turn, can contribute to the well-being of whole communities and countries."

– *Kofi Annan*

My earliest recollection of football was watching my hero Bryan Robson orchestrating a resounding 3-0 win against an all star Barcelona team at Old Trafford in the European Cup Winners Cup quarter finals in 1984. Other significant memories include Liverpool beating AS Roma in the European Cup final that year with Bruce Grobbelaar's 'wobbly legs' clown antics cementing his place in footballing folklore, Everton capturing the Cup Winners Cup against Rapid Wien in 85 and the Liverpool double year of 1986.

As a ten year old, the icing on the cake was Mexico 86, which was just an incredible and endless talent show; El Diego, Preben Elkjær, Laudrup, Francescoli, Scotland's shorts, Michel Platini, Zico, Butragueno, Negrete, Sanchez, Belanov and Lineker. For a starry eyed youngster, this was a mesmerising tournament, one which cemented an obsession with the beautiful game.

I started writing football poems in 2006 after I stumbled across a football poetry website. Most of these poems and the inspiration behind them have been penned on the go, waiting in a queue, driving, whilst listening to a lecture etc.

During the 2005 World Summit, global Governments acknowledged that "sports can foster peace and development, and can contribute to an atmosphere of tolerance and understanding" and the evidence is there. Through football we can promote peace, tolerance and celebration of diversity. Poetry is a medium to express inspiration and creativity, it is a portal for ingenuity and inventiveness to thrive and for talent to be celebrated and prosper and I have jumped on the bandwagon and readily signed up as a member.

The reader is requested to bear in mind that I do this as a hobby and wrote this book to share my pastime with likeminded football fans. Any constructive criticism is much sought and will be taken on board.

Emdad

THE GREATEST GAME ON EARTH

"One generation plants the trees; another gets the shade."
— Chinese Proverb

El Diego's boots

A dream come true
One that constantly replayed and had been easy to construe

Oh what a glorious day of sunshine it had been
The savings box emptied my smile stretched, from Bognor to Berlin

I realised that the moment was close, When I would be the proud owner of a Diego boot
You see I was the barrel chested one's latest fanclub recruit

Sprinting down to the Whitechapel Road I dragged me Mam
Dropping a shopping bag en route, breaking a jar of strawberry jam

"You wear them, you'll play like him" the shop assistant said
I believed every word as my beaming smile spread

A walking Ambassador I became, oh did I put those boots to use
On grass, tarmac and concrete, there was many a bruise

"Wear the boots," a voice said, "and the class will ooze"
The old sandpitch on the Berner Estate

Not ideal for that surface, but that was open to debate
Even wore them to school on an odd day or three

"Get them off," a hawkeyed Margaret wailed like a banshee
Dream is all I did as I wore them with honour

Yes the one and only Puma Maradona.

© **Emdad Rahman**

Glorious Maradona! A dream replayed by millions.

Hot air bag

Who'd have thought that a bag of hot air

Would entertain a billion?

A day would come when the bag juggler's flair

Would set Chairmen back a cool million

Who would have thought that a bag of hot air

Could also cause much misery?

War breaks out, Honduras and El Salvador

Proof the pictures not all colourful and shimmery

Who would have thought that a bag of hot air

Would dominate countless a schoolboy dream

Bulging stadia with all the fanfare

All frenzily cheering on their team

So to all who are there or in a comfy armchair

Lets preserve our love of this bag of hot air.

© **Emdad Rahman**

No prizes for guessing what's being described.

Remembering Wharton

A black pearl on an ivory beach

The first to extend his reach

Paved the way gloriously, Three Degrees, Blissett, Barnes, Earle and Wright

The Sassenach who would highlight the black man's plight

At Stamford the Lilywhite set a hundred metre record

Racism saw to it that there was no England cap award

With authority the Blades penalty area the ex Miller would stalk

Until competition arrived in the rotund shape of "fatty" Foulke

Died in 1930 as a penniless alcoholic

Yet his memory remains rather vitriolic

Wright Phillips, Lennon, Richards and Bent

Let us all remember Wharton, he with the foreign accent.

© **Emdad Rahman**

Wharton, the forerunner was the world record holder for the 100 yard dash and most likely the first African to play professional cricket in Britain. Wharton achieved greatness during Victorian England. His achievements are further outstanding considering he lived during a murky period of history where black people were treated as the lowest of the low.

Birchfield Harrier Wharton, dubbed the best goalkeeper in the North of England, excelled in a number of sports. His talent was contrary to

popular perceptions of black inferiority and it is a wonder as to why he is for the most part overlooked today.

Bust that onion bag

What a scintillating feeling when the ball hits the net

Conjured up through sheer blood, tears and sweat

Penalty precision

Six yard box incision

Spectacular free kick

Huh! The wall lost a brick

Forty yard piledriver

All a part of moments to savour

Or even the Goalie's punt

That could be saved by my Aunt

As time becomes slow motion it adds up to one emotion

A universal ecstatic sensation.

© **Emdad Rahman**

The cocking of the trigger, the release, bang, whiz, the net bulges, slow motion as the roar amplifies. Ecstasy!

Dirt free Harry

Harry Redknapp, shrewd operator, underrated footballing brain

Attractive teams playing delightful football without refrain

The master of suspense, enjoys a flutter

A maverick like Clough, with a bit of a splutter

In an age of obsession for pure English stock

He'd be a genius for the national team, an East End Hitchcock.

© **Emdad Rahman**

Harry, Barry Fry, Jim Smith. They don't make them like they used to. Harry is part of a dying breed, although I prefer the new age Managers. He'll never be England boss because he's a live grenade who'd never get on with the executives at the FA.

Evertonian ecstasy

Congratulations to Everton for winning the Champions League final

All eleven hungry toffees fought like the Royal Bengal

In earthly terms, what is termed as the two hundred and fourth Merseyside derby

Saw David Moyes elevated to the status of Sir Matt Busby

Johnson's brace led to a stunning rout

Even though the Reds performed like limp sauerkraut

"For us to concede three is not right," Benitez said

With bigger fish to fry, it's safe to say the Reds will still finish ahead.

© **Emdad Rahman**

Merseyside derby: 09.09.06. Times must hard when a Mersey derby win is celebrated with such vigour! It says it all about the gulf between the two Mersey giants.

'Lurch' makes history

History is a byword at Wembley

Where once Dave Beasant made history

Clive Goodyear clumsily upends the great Aldo

A textbook predator with the precision of Nick Faldo

Pheet! Penalty! A monumental piece of history has just taken place

The disappointment etched vividly on every Don face

The Wembley turf heaves, every single blade

Eleven penalties in the bag, Aldo gets ready to raid

A master craftsman fires left, firm, sidefooted,

It's a glorious day in May

Ninety eight thousand dumbstruck as Mayonnaise man palms the ball away

Did I say history is a byword at Wembley

Where once Dave Beasant made history.

© **Emdad Rahman**

Let us not forget the Lurch also helped Chelsea lift the ZDS Cup at Wembley.

Jumping Jackflashes

Klinsmann said to Johnson; "Nosedive and retire,
Just like a stricken spitfire."

Rivaldo said to Rojas; "Use the blade, let some skin part,
And hit the deck like a wayward dart."

Paolo said to Alcock; "I'll push, you pirouette like a dancing Shaikh,
We'll do our very own rendition of Swan Lake."

Not to be outdone, Ronaldo said to Robben; "For the panto we'll fancy dress,
And have the last laugh over Ortega and Pires."

Divers, the villains of the football panto
Make or break, for a friend or foe

The worst the guilty get is a ban or a fine
Or for artistic excellence, a credible nine point nine.

© **Emdad Rahman**

I actually left out the most notorious, Laurent Blanc's best mate Slaven Bilic.

Schole in the hole

The most timid individual you could ever hope to meet

With limelight shunning Scholesey it's always discreet

But on the battlefield, in the Ginger ninja's pursuit of glory

Wayward tackles are parcel of his glorious life story

Whether it's a failed uppercut, bite, elbow, stamp or knuckle

You can count on the wizard's tackling prowess provoking many a chuckle.

© **Emdad Rahman**

This maestro has simply been the best midfielder in the country for a number of years. Interesting, considering he started off as a striker. Some of his goals have simply been sublime. Despite that, gentleman Scholes remains one of the most down to earth, publicity shunning superstar in world football. He retired from the international scene at a good time, as his position in the team at the time was questioned by many. The extra rest has paid dividends for United.

Marc Vivien Foe   1975 – 2003

A giant of a man, gentleness personified

Braveheart, graceful, striking smile

True ambassador of everything exquisite about the beautiful game

The family of football shattered by this loss

A part of football died in Lyon that day

Lost, but not forgotten.

© **Emdad Rahman**

A tragic loss of a great man as well as a brilliant footballer.

A summer's night in Istanbul

The Ataturk hosts two colossal giants of the game
Liverpool and Milan get set for universal acclaim

Typical Traore foul, arms flailing, a human windmill
Evergreen Maldini fires in from the resulting cross, blast it's one nil

Deathly silence, the makeshift Kop are silenced
Nonsense! It's only a temporary form of grievance

Liverpool, Liverpool is the chant
Above all other anthems can be heard this descant

Milan again thrust forward, the hapless Djimi beaten
Semi revenge for Chelsea as Crespo unlocks the dungeon
Ooh! The cups heading to Milan for certain

The groans can be heard from Toxteth to Berlin
The Red stagecoach is fast turning into a pumpkin

Kaka breaks, the killer ball as Crespo applies the coup de grace
Cruel! Istanbul Reds seek cover and pray for solace

"Game over" screams Andy Gray as my Dad, storms out in disgust
Milan are the epitome of magnificence, majestic epitome and august

The HT whistle is welcomed like a long lost brother
Dreams wrecked cruelly, lying neglected in a smother

The Rafalution is over, the Scousers are heartbroke
We need a Rafa moment of genius, a master stroke

This is not one memory the Reds will evoke
As Didi Hamann emerges in the shape of a baroque

Second half, Dudek magically defies a Shevchenko free kick
This, the defining moment when proceedings become toxic

Two crosses from Riise, the second precisely onto the head of a pin
Stevie G, marauding, grandiose, masterful leaps to head in

Captain fantastic jerks his arms, "Come on!" is the scream
A banner says, "Stevie is bigger than the Beatles!", will they dare to blaspheme?

Didi now feeds a blood hungry Vlad the Impaler
Skimmed shot, edge of the box, demise reports a failure

It's fever pitch now, strangers are holding each other crying
If I said my arm hairs weren't standing I'd probably be lying

Our own Milan backheels to give Gerrard the freedom of the town
Oh the Milan agony as General Gattuso hacks him down

Alonso steps up, Dida stretches left, misses
Ecstasy though with the resultant rebound, "get in there" he hisses

It's cardiac arrest time, football's greatest comeback... thus far
The fans go into overdrive in this Turkish bazaar

Injury time finishes, extra time begins, Smicer suffers a cramp hit
Carra suffers the same fate, valiant clearance to acquit
The trick is repeated a minute later, what price this spirit?

AC cross, Shevchenko heads, Jerzy saves a la Banks
Straight to feet though, Sheva fires home, still balanced on the gangplank

Disbelief as replays show the missile deflected over
Final whistle, I visualise Red fans tottering on the cliffs of Dover

Penalties and Liverpool have stuck a Pole in the goal
It's our very own Jerzy, straight from the Mersey

Serginho shoots into orbit, endangering low flying birds
This is not part of the script, it's all rather absurd

Didi puts one beyond Dida's wave
As Pirlo's lame effort is saved

The Lord of Frodsham sends Dida hurtling aimlessly into a canyon
Tomasson at last blasts one home in retaliation

Riise of all people misses as Kaka beats Grobbelaar reincarnated
The Impaler sends Dida the wrong way as football's breath is bated

Jerzy dives right but palms the ball back out in a moment which is sublime
Yes Liverpool are European Champions for the fifth time

I end this pome here as the party hits Sputnik
To dear Istanbul we bid Allaha Ismarladýk.

© Emdad Rahman

Diego Maradona said, "Even the Brazil team that won the 1970 World Cup could not have staged a comeback with Milan leading 3-0."

My Dad is a diehard Gooner. He stormed out to the Mosque after Liverpool went three down. When he returned the score was 3-3. I could hear my Sister telling him the score in the corridor and heard him tell her off for her prank...... Priceless.... The rest is history.

Video nasty!

Coming soon to a stadium near you, Steve Round Productions brings you a cracker

Roll up for an exclusive screening, of the Old Trafford Chainsaw Massacre

Pre match fans nerves, would it be a dour draw or a goal spree?

But on the pitch the poor lambs got their little boots clogged in ghee

As defeat to Espana led to a horror DVD

Starring – Benny from Watford, upon sighting the ball he fled

Arms flailing wildly ala Dawn of the dead

Good old G Neville played himself as shop steward

Nasty after game comments had him well and truly skewered

Villa reduced Rio to an imitation of The Wicker Man

Nightmare on Elm Street, screamed the boisterous Stretford clan

Woody the mad axe murderer looked like he'd emerged from a pond

Pinged useless long balls, all into The Beyond

Dependable P Neville's return seemed like a horrid dream

No left sided option left viewers wanting to Scream

Stevie G starred as England's Chief Kaiser

More starring roles for the reformed Hellraiser
A non show from Carricko, does Ray Wilkins still exist?

Can't help with your gaping expressions mate, you need an Exorcist

"I can play with Stevie" Lamps was Les Diaboliques

How we all pine for his ruthless goal streak

Boy blunder Phillips epitomised crosses to Vampyr

Ninety more minutes and he would've threatened to perspire

Crouchie had things on mind, had he forgotten the rent?

As Iniesta's strike pushed England into The Descent

Wonderboy Dyer had Roeder of the North East scowling

Pity the rest of the nation were left Howling

On a bleak night Macca's men failed to enthral

Twelve horror flicks mentioned in this pome, can you spot them all?

© **Emdad Rahman**

After the February 2007 defeat to Spain at Old Trafford, England Coach Steve McClaren sent his players statistical data analysis and tailor-made DVDs of their individual performances. Macca vowed that every player would be held "accountable."

Monsieur Wenger's Rage

A s the family of football hail him a footballing Professor
R ed rages, not the norm with Monsieur Wenger
S uccess, a byword of the mercurial one's career
E xuding sparkling mineral water, not so the traditional beer
N ever have we seen him so animated as against the Claret
E nvy and rage had him reaching for a heavy fleurette
W est Ham, a place where passion runs en bloc
E njoin and agree, Professeur's emotions ran amok
N ow the time he did his best Mourinho impersonation
G reat story for the hacks, gleefully scribbling with jubilation
E nd this farce scream the blazer brigade
R eal fans pray this witch hunt's not a point scoring crusade.

© **Emdad Rahman**

The 2006/07 season saw Monsieur Wenger's display rage like never before. Has the Professor's cool streak changed? Has the studious Jekyll become Hyde?

Little & Large Show

Keegan and Toshack, one big, one small

Dynamic duo that never failed to enthral

A trademark knockdown, flick

Followed by a concise finish, click

Could Torres and Kuyt repeat the heroics of the past

But will their telepathy ever be as fast

An iconic twosome who made defenders pray

As the mighty Red wave swept all in their way.

© **Emdad Rahman**

See Bellamy and Crouch.

The Major's last stand

Who's the fat chap they said as he strolled out at Wembley
"Who the hell are Hungary?," cold hands are rubbed in glee

The greatest purveyors of the art, England from planet football
A heavy lesson expected as Hungary enter the assembly hall.

They absolutely routed the English, old timers recall
Made to look like the condemned, legless on a pub crawl

They sang the skipper was the fat porker, squat, one foot, no pace
Just as the left cannon exploded, exploiting the airtight space

As the Wembley massacre took effect, strict precision and military service
The awesome Billy Wright was reduced to an absolute novice

Thus Roly Poly's Incredibles became the first victorious foreigners at Wembley

As the mighty England were hammered, six goals to three

His girth and ungainly gait led to the tag of 'Galloping Major'
After this demolition job he was no longer to be a stranger

His death leaves the fondest of memories amidst all the strife
Simply one of the greatest players that I have seen in my life.

© **Emdad Rahman**

Ferenc Puskás: 1927-2006

"That one game alone changed our thinking. We thought we would demolish this team... we are the masters, they are the pupils. It was absolutely the other way... the game had a profound effect, not just on myself but all of us... Ferenc Puskás changed my life."
– Sir Bobby Robson.

FC Carra & Gerry

If it weren't for Jamie and Steven where would the Pool be?
Would they lose to Tranmere, odd goal in three

Vital solder in the squad, one very low in esteem
The single vital image of Rafa's regime

"Also rans, has beens" do we hear the mancs shout
Fergie'll have them in a jiffy, that'll smite your trout pout

As Scouseland dream of their own Desert Storm
Let that thought keep all Liverpudlian hearts, toasted and warm.

© **Emdad Rahman**

The backbone and bedrock of the Liverpool dominance.

Wanderers Wonderland

Wanderers, destroyers of footballing dreams

Allardyce's infantry will run you out of steam

An eclectic mix of mercenaries, bargains and journeymen

Lost causes? They all rejuvenate in Big Sam's den

Not quite Wimbledon but you get the drift

They'll grind you, and hurt you, execution is swift

The European Cup may be the holy grail

Bolton in the Champions league? Maybe when I'm frail

You call them hoofers, too physical, an unfashionable team

But hey in a democracy everyone can dream.

© **Emdad Rahman**

Note: Big Sam has since moved onto the hot seat at Newcastle. Time will tell how successful he is.

The silent king

He is Brother Abdul Salam Bilal from Versailles
His career has surfaced the high points all the way

Still a footballing nomad as time elapses on the clock
Presently he's comfortably nestled up north in the Reebok

This A list footballer commenced his career at PSG
Before leaving for North London, hopping across the sea

Goal blitz under the Professor's tutelage, North London toasted him with glee
Soon jetted to Madrid in a record breaking fee

Not before he'd put many a Premier defence to the sword
Winning plaudits galore and the young player award

An enigma you may say of exceptional ability
Monsieur has always chosen not to settle in one city

Paris, Liverpool, the blue half of Manchester and Turkey
Will the Wanderer demand a transfer in January?

A much maligned and misunderstood enigma
Brother Abdul Salam, please remember us in your prayer

Back in Blighty, Bilal will continue to do the biz
You'll not get any points for guessing who he is.

© **Emdad Rahman**

Arsene Wenger's best ever discovery as Vieira was already a star at Milan. A much maligned enigma. Even Thierry Henry did not show the same promise Anelka showed as a youngster. Thus far his badly advised career has not reached the heights it should have.

Poland's Montgomery – Acrostic homage to Dudek!

D espite the frantic fanfare, time froze
U p popped a balletically poised gloved hand
D udek of the woolly Jerzy variety
E cstasy as realisation dawns, time unfreezes
K op shrieks of frenzy can be heard all through the Istanbul night.

© **Emdad Rahman**

"At the end of extra time, Jamie Carragher came over and told me to remember Bruce Grobbelaar's spaghetti legs against Roma in 1984. 'Do the same as Grobbelaar, dance, do anything, put them off,' he said."
– *Jerzy Dudek in an interview with the Independent.*

No fan will ever forget the night of 25th May 2005. Thank you Jerzy.

The devil incarnate

What kind of monster uses a golf club on a fellow pro
Blame the drink and nervously wipe your brow

When will Bellamy the buffoon come to his sense?
If he's kicked out of Anfield, he'll be permanently on the fence

With the Gillette and Hicks revolution getting ready to load
For some this may very well be the end of the road.

© **Emdad Rahman**

Bellamy: Brilliant talent with a touch of nasty!

Redemption

Dreams galore in the Cathedral Nou Camp, but who will fulfil?
It's Enzo Bearzot's squadra Azzurra against Tele Santanaâ's Brazil

A Blue victory is a must, their fate finely balanced on a seesaw
Red hot favourites Brazil though would go through with a draw

Living artists ply their wares, Socrates, Eder, Falcao, Cerezo
For Barcelona see Sao Paolo, El Jogo Bonito

But trouble seems to lurk in paradise, a hungry assassin primed for a redeeming hit
Cool, calm and ice cool hitman Rossi clamps his teeth around the bit

Two years in the wilderness, surely he's nothing but a misfit
No goals as yet the cynics say, will he ever acquit?

Twenty two master craftsmen serve up one of the best matches ever
A stinging hat trick from an avenging Rossi, never say never

Three flashes of brilliance, from criminal to darling of the nation
As a nation erupts we hear, a muffled scream, redemption.

© **Emdad Rahman**

The unlikely hero of Espana 82. For the modern see David Beckham.

Iron man or Psycho

An attack as such would get you arrested for Grievous Bodily Harm

What went through Thatcher's head, a raging bull before, a horrendous smash with the forearm

And where was Dermot G, unsighted, poor and acrid

Such deliberate and violent acts cannot be tolerated

Will Big Ben turn it round to win back his adored acclaim?

Works cut, after the most horrible challenge ever seen in the game

Will he return, bright, sparkly and bristly

Or will secluded reflection make him a menace to society

He's a nice chap and many will wish him well

The ball's in your court Thatch; reform or rebel.

© **Emdad Rahman**

Ben Thatcher's horror tackle on Pedro Mendes. What was going through his head, and such a nice guy away off the pitch...

Sweet Liverpool

Liverpool win three on the trot

Eleven goals, wow they're hot

A poor phase, followed by a blistering streak

Now can we keep it going week after week

We can go places says Rafa the Sage

As the form book declines before the turn of the page

Losing streak hits home as the Reds are overturned

Normal service resumed as far as I'm concerned

Istanbul brilliance, consistency we rue

Oh Liverpool we love you!

© **Emdad Rahman**

Probably the greatest team on the planet.

Cashley Cole

The yawn saga involving Cashley Cole
Was he egged on by Cheryl Tweedy?
To the devil he sold his worthless soul
The lure of a third Bentley left him very needy

It remains to be seen if Cash jumps ship when Barca wag a finger?
In his quest for silver, will fans contemplate letting him off the hook?
Fat chance they'll get as he'll be off too quick with a swipe of his left stinger
Whilst strolling into the sunset with his glorious trophy minger

What folly! Just a self obsessed nonentity
And when Corporal Mourinho smacks his bottom, he'll leave Chelski in the lurch
"It's all their fault," he'll whine, "I'm just a little nobody from the city"
Leaving once again, a reputation sullied, soiled, besmirched

Acquisitiveness and criticism of colleagues was oh not so clever
A time will come when this piece of detail could damn him forever.

© **Emdad Rahman**

Arsene Wenger nurtured this fellow. He repaid that by stabbing him in the back.

Il Capitano of the Nerazzuri

Poise, elegance, nobility and a regal air dominated his rule
Recollections of the sixties Inter team brings about a beaming smile
A rare and prolific defender who never lost his cool
Just an amazing epitome of grace and style

Make no mistake this is Giacinto Fachetti
Atlanta bound, reigned in by Herrara for Inter's full back slot
Monopolised enterprising cutting runs like a sharpened machete
Defended the rearguard with the fervour of a zealot

Seria A, Euro and Intercontinental trophies by the bagful
His death leaves a lamentable vacuum
Inter aficionados will feel the pangs when the heart strings pull
Stadio Meazza memories of the Emperor will become a footballing heirloom

Cabrini, Baresi, Maldini all clones of the boy from Treviglio
The legacy lives on within the art of Catenaccio.

© **Emdad Rahman**

The greatest fullback ever.

Davide Pleate

The problem with David Pleat

Begins when he starts to bleat

Not a pundit I'd particularly like to meet

As his voice reminds me of steel on sleet

His analysis leaves one deadbeat

His sentences are rarely complete

Have you heard his verbal mincemeat?

Lord help us when it's an England defeat

Tactical talk leaves me deadbeat

After ITV promise a footy treat

A headcheck may reveal concrete

Remember the jigging Kenilworth Road athlete?

Idiosyncratic pronunciation of surnames is so offbeat

Just a dinosaur who is obsolete.

© **Emdad Rahman**

Jokes aside, this guy amazed me with his Spurs team of 1987. Third in the league and runners up at Wembley. Waddle, Hoddle and Allen were on fire. Why did he leave?

And Sheva must score...

Shevchenko, living legend, launches the gaping goal seeking missile

Jumping bullfrog Jerzy jumps a mile

In unison the makeshift Kop scream "save"

Unfortunate rebound, surely a goal as Sheva lines up the second wave

And Sheva must score... Attack, attack, attack!

Collective gasp, it must be a mirage as aghast the world stands aback

"Woe unto me" roars Sheva

What followed will remain in the annals of history forever.

© **Emdad Rahman**

Bruce Grobbelaar eat your heart out!

The Laird from Govan

Fergie, Fergie

A catatonic burst of energy

You'll do well if you're St Neville of the clergy

Be Ruud, avoid him like the lergy

Strachan became a hypersensitive reaction to an allergy

Same fate for Brian Kidd, a man of Panergy

Big time Ince, a pure definition of Surgy

Aussie Mark Bosnich, a mixed bag of lethargy

Spice boy Greening, shipped off to be a Baggy

With Becks it was turning into a big showbiz orgy

A brilliant stopper in Stam, but not working in synergy

With delusional Yorkey the picture was getting muggy

Last straw for Lieutenant Keano, were things getting foggy?

Cross him and the resulting taste will be tangy

New dawn with the Fergie babes, get ready with the buggy

Many will come and go, but the Govan Don will always remain the biggie.

© **Emdad Rahman**

Don Ferguson: The Godfather of world football.

Gladiator Tardelli's Passion

The peak of football, finale Espana nineteen hundred and eight two

And maybe for once Paolo Rossi is not the darling of this pome

The efficient Germans line-up against a rejuvenated blue

Azurri, Azurri! All roads lead to Rome

We speak of the warrior Tardelli

Whom Fifa describe as the complete Italian midfielder

Who scored before Altobelli

And became a global superstar

Sixty ninth minute, Bergomi passes into the hole

A slide shot, with no bend

Like a heat seeking missile, goal!

What ensued has become ingrained into legend

Tears streaming, chest thumping, roaring, the opposition forlorn

For the unromantic Schumacher things look very lean

This isn't a memory that fades the next morn

Not the look of a professional but the realisation of a boyhood dream

The raw, unbridled joy in unrevised celebration

Yes, pure unadulterated joy can be mean

Has there ever been so much emotion?

Quite simply the best goal celebration ever seen.

© **Emdad Rahman**

A man in ecstasy. Repeated by Fabio Grosso in the Italy V Germany 2006 semi finals.

Red Army!

The Catalan roadshow had arrived
Deco, Puyol, Eto
A masterful plan Rijkaard had contrived
Giuly, Messi, Ronaldinho

They came to town amidst much fanfare
But FC Carra and Gerry law await
"They're a glorified long ball team" the coach would declare
Hoping Sir Benitez would take the bait

Is that a faint tremor we hear reverberating around Europe?
As Gerry Marsden's trumpet is blown
Victory pushes the Reds up the slope
You'll never walk alone

Has an Anfield defeat been celebrated with such vigour
As the masterful Eider sticks the knife in again
Yes, famous Anfield European nights are again de rigueur
But for Europe's kings there's no more champagne

"Bring it on" screams the skipper as to a wave of joy, the Red Army all succumb
Sir Benitez arise is the heralded announcement! Athens here we come!

© **Emdad Rahman**

Liverpool V Barcelona: Anfield - 06/03/07.

Blunt Macca

They call him Mac the knife

With a new found temperament much suited to Fife

New white teeth, big smile, his chic is not boho

Though thoroughly approved by the men from Soho

Becks was one of the best of his generation

Axed by Moustache Pete Mac and his delegation

What happens if Lennon or SWP are out

We'll see the strength of this new found clout

Questions not answered by a thumping of Greece

Will the team wilt under pressure and start to crease,

In the run up to Euro two thousand and eight

A stuttering qualification and he's out through the gate

I fear the new England boss

May be seen as someone who served up a load of dross

And when his one track tactic stalls

He'll be seen as just a mouthpiece of Lord Terence of Venables.

© **Emdad Rahman**

Penned way before Goldenballs comeback. Welcome back Becks.

Professor screwball and his madcap boots

A Norseman set sail for England
The most successful manager in Norway ever
The Dons of Wimbledon he took command
Purveyors of kick, rush, brawn, endeavour

'He reminds me of Wenger', said the Earl with adore
'We burnt his boots after a game, he just laughed and said he had four more.'

As big Sam Hammam pronounced a managerial coup
The boot clad Marxist left everyone feeling quite blue
'I only want to manage Wimbledon or Brazil' he had said
But Wellington boots, were never likely to be the way ahead

In the end the eccentric chose to leave, with money safely in the bank
Better that way because it was only a matter of time, he was made to walk the plank.

© **Emdad Rahman**

Drillo's methods are now known as sports science. Mourinho and Allardyce swear by it.

The Lisbon Lions

The Lisbon Lions who ran
Never a team in tow
They matched Internazionale man to man
All born in touching distance of Glasgow

Cappellini felled by Craig,
Mazzola fires in the pen
Inter retreat into a cocoon like defence
As it looks much like boys versus men

Gemmell levels from Craig's pass into space
Murdoch's shot deflected by Chalmers to score
The crowd bay for the countdown race
As the Lions get ready to roar

History, as the Bhoys hold on in Lisbon town
Thus becoming the first Brits to lift the European crown.

© **Emdad Rahman**

All the triumphant Lions were home bred, born within a 30 mile radius of Glasgow.

The Iceman

Named in tribute to Denis law

Dennis Maria Bergkamp, he came he saw

Sublime Arsenal legend, folk hero

Through the high times and the low

Serving Ajax, Inter and the Gunners with distinction

Out of this world artistry, vision with precision

A class act, in the true sense of the word

Zola, Cantona, Henry, he puts them all to the sword

Never quite conquered a fear of flying

Aviophobia? Till retirement he kept trying

For a second let's forget all the twaddle

And reflect on the protégé of Glen Hoddle

The Gunners own Chrissie Waddle?

Proving once and for all, his genius was not a doddle

The Dutch Master, Beavis, Bergy, Iceman screamed the Highbury banners

As the non flying Dutchman took them on a quest of honours

Goal of the month, one, two, three

Poor Nikos Dabizas and Leicester City

Recognition for gracing football so long

He modernised the Premiership and helped make it so strong

It's a crime he won't grace the Emirates

Cometh the hour, cometh the menace

Thanks for proving footballs not tennis

He'll always be to the normal fan

The Dutch Master, Beavis, Bergy, Iceman.

© **Emdad Rahman**

Deft touches, silky flicks, precision passing and killer finishing. A master craftsman.

The Magnificent Magyars

The great Stanley Mathews summed it up like a beautiful day's weather

"They are the best team I ever played against. They were the best ever."

Known as Aranycsapatin in Hungary, they played football with the lyre

The golden team to you and me, musicians amidst the pyre

Led by Ferenc Puskas, marauding Real Madrid hero, the galloping Major

Record goalscorer of all time, never will he be a stranger

Hidegkuti probing, making space in the hole

The first exponent of the deep lying centre forward role

Zoltan Czibor with the accuracy of a wild west gunslinger

Wing wizardry, the legacy of an all time great left winger

Then there was Boszik, graceful midfielder, a golden beacon and beam

A cultured playmaker, full of steam, the brains behind the team

Grosics took on the mantle of a revolutionary new role

The archetypal second sweeper, the heartbeat and the soul

Lorant the sweeper with flowing attacks brimming with power

An example so perfected by Kaiser Beckenbauer

We move onto the marauding right back, the steely Buzanszky

Express train, bulletlike, young and free!

Lantos working simultaneously, a busy bee on the left

Sizzling pace, startling grace, leaving opposing teams bereft

Zakarias the defensive midfielder calmly policing his rounds

In today's market he'd be worth at least eighteen million pounds

Budai on the right, on a steed he'd be a knight

Tracking up and down, in and out, by golly he gave teams a fright

Kocsis nicknamed goldenhead for his aerial power

Indomitable Golden Boot winner, an irresolute tower

Fifty four world cup heralds the Olympic champions, all ready to slay

A long unbeaten run, they'll blow all in their path away

A nine nil victory over South Korea, a West German massacre eight goals to three

The mighty Hungarians are in town, the travelling support are full of glee

The Magicians arrive on the back of a four-year unbeaten run

The miracle result in the final saw the Magyars undone

Brazil and Uruguay like dirty rags on the scrapheap, tossed to a side

The march goes on and it seems that nothing will spoil the ride

But don't understate German party poopers, proficient with the proverbial 'boo'

Helmut Rahn knocks in a brace as Fritz Walters men triumph three two.

© **Emdad Rahman**

The Hungarian revolution of 1956 spelt the demise of one of the greatest teams of all time. The uprising started as players from Honved were returning from a match against Atletico Bilbao. Players like Puskás, Czibor and Kocsis chose to stay in Western Europe and never played for Hungary again.

Fergie's bridesmaids

They blamed it on the weather
Said the surface was to wet
Milan went hell for leather
The memory evokes a cold sweat

As Kaka had a blaster
Roo and Ron went missing
A lesson from the master
That left Laird Fergie hissing

At the end of the day
The devils lost their bottle
To Vidic's dismay
Gattuso charged at full throttle

You may have Gary Neville, smug fans, all the cash
Milan turn up, it's all gone in a flash.

© **Emdad Rahman**

The brawn of Gattuso defeated the beauty of Ronaldo.

Athens 2007

A re football legions in for another treat
T he stadia of Europe heave, ho, shudder and greet
H uyton gets ready to unleash its forces
E nd the reign of pretenders, no time for discourses
N ew recruits will ensure the Reds supreme reign
S urely not the champions of Europe again?

© **Emdad Rahman**

Pre Athens 2007.

Reversing fortune

Rueing missed chances,
defensive lapses,
lost opportunities
If only...

© **Emdad Rahman**

It's easy when you look back in hindsight.

Gross judgemental error

By tube he arrived at White Hart Lane

Brandishing a travel card, signalling the beginning of a tumultuous reign

The saviour who would again make the mighty cockerel crow

You see this once mighty club had reached an all time low

"I vill bring back the glory days," the mood was bullish

As the faithful licked their lips with utmost relish

But the Gross reign was the personification of a full scale disaster

The cracks were deep, more was needed than just plaster

A respectable reputation earned at Grasshoppers Zurich

All burnt to cinders like a wayward match flick

His outbursts singled him out as a modern day king kong

At least he bought back Klinsmann for a final swansong

With regards to his Hollywood looks, many were not keen

Realistically, he would never grace the cover of GQ magazine

In short Herr Gross had proved to be a belligerently lost cube

As he was sent packing, of course on the tube.

© Emdad Rahman

The absence of Fritz Schmid, his right hand man was a blow. Underrated Gross restored some respectability with his FC Basel team that stormed the Swiss league, whilst causing damage in the champions league against British clubs.

Athina 2007

As we herald in the clash of two modern day titans
Beware of a port city's Red clan bearing gifts
The dawn of Rafa's Iliad will be reborn and enlighten
The Attica Periphary of Central Greece

Did you know that the Trojan horse was actually a Greek mare?
As Liverpool look set to reclaim their rightful crown
As the Milanese will discover, blinded by a powerful Red flair
Leaving with nothing but a rueful frown

As Liverpool will unleash Achilles
The cradle of civilisation will be raving mad
A giant of the Trojan war will be unleashed on the sweet breeze
By the most magnificent warrior of Rafael's Iliad

The historic ancient Agora will see no Achilles heel
As in the shade of the Acropolis, victory the Reds will seal.

© **Emdad Rahman**

Penned 15 minutes before the kickoff: Athina.

> *Nought from the Greeks towards me hath sped well.*
> *So now I find that ancient proverb true,*
> *Foes' gifts are no gifts: profit bring they none.*
>
> *Sophocles (496 - 406 BC), Ajax*

In case you haven't figured... Achilles = Gerrard

Milanese hit Haiku

dominant reds reigned
milanese hit on the break
viva Inzaghi

© **Emdad Rahman**

Sums the match up perfectly. If Liverpool had a finisher they'd have won at a canter. The difference was the predator Inzaghi.

Allemagne Acrostic

G ermany, write them off at your peril
E veryone I know did, including my friend Cheryl
R unning teams ragged with games full of wonder
M arks, get set, go. A Phillip Lahm bolt of thunder
A nd it was only then we began to wonder, that
N ews of their demise had been greatly exaggerated
Y es, the team that everyone once hated

W orld cup winners 54, 74 and 90
R unners up thrice, including a classic with Blighty
I nto extra time did they go in 66
T he Russian linesman Bakhramov, they swore it was a fix
E ngland triumphant once, but there was no repeat for years

T he Germans continued to triumph and all we had were tears
H ark the Olympic Stadium, doom and gloom with Jancker
E mily Heskey beating Kahn, ensuring he'd had a stinker
M ade the defence look paperweight, in particular Thomas Linke

O verath, Beckenbaur, Seeler, Netzer, all time stars who rock
F rings, Podolski, Lahm, Borowski, new kids on the block
F or all those who doubted, the chapter had closed

A llemagne at home, the team rose and rose
T he public couldn't believe, an Azurri thrashing had them torn

Y es, yes, yes the was the chorus, champagne football was the norm
O ut were the shackles once the tournament began
U ber alles became the norm and the beer ran and ran
R iproaring attack sent the Swedes on their way

P enalties against the Argies, ole, ole, ole
E nd of the semi nears, penalties again on the horizon
R oaring Del Piero sends the Azurri into oblivion
I nto the sunset strides California Klinsmann on his trusty steed
L ow now heralds in an exciting chapter, which I for one can't wait to read.

© **Emdad Rahman**

The Germans playing without any fear was the highlight of a drab world cup for me. The group stages were great, but after that things petered out. Klinsmann's team were a joy to watch and provided great entertainment and drama throughout. The organisation of the tournament was pure German. Beckenbauer seemed to have been cloned, as he was everywhere.

Brilliant Orange

Brilliant Orange

Schizophrenic they may be

Two world cup final losses,

Leaving the nation all at sea

'Total Voetbal,' switching positions with ease

Flowing passes, stubborn possession, the killer pass, all a breeze

Wilkes, Cruyff, Gullit to name but three

Stars for the future include Van Persie

The future is orange, the future is bright

The spirit of Rembrandt and Van Gogh is truly alight.

© **Emdad Rahman**

In a nutshell... "The neurotic genius of Dutch football"

David Winner

Combat with Lawro

Camp Lawro! It's debatable whether he's the best pundit on screen

Fun to watch though, when he vents his spleen

I met him once at a charity event

Great Ormond's footy funday, I was sent off for dissent

The golden ticket footy match

A superstar XI, a plan we needed to hatch

Lawro, Ray Stubbs, Nigel Pearson

If we won I promised I'd do the 'Merson'

A 50/50 ball

Too close to call

Both feet up, mind the gap

I ended up in poor Lawro's lap

Sheer agony! It became clear I'd hit him where it hurt

A young girl screamed at me, I hid my head in my shirt

Red card! Head up, I trudged off graceful as a swan

A heartbeat later the final whistle, hurrah we'd won!

© **Emdad Rahman**

I've been very descriptive, but this actually happened.

Printed in the United Kingdom
by Lightning Source UK Ltd.
121641UK00002B/151-198/A